Gambol the World:
Eine Weltanschauung

New and selected poems
by Silvia Kofler

Kansas City — Spartan Press — Missouri

Spartan Press
Kansas City, Missouri
spartanpresskc.com

Copyright (c) Silvia Kofler, 2017
First Edition 1 3 5 7 9 10 8 6 4 2
ISBN: 978-1-946642-17-2
LCCN: 2017941112

Design, edits and layout: Jason Ryberg
Author photo and cover painting: Dave Paarmann
All rights reserved. No part of this publication may be reproduced or transmitted in any form or by any means, electronic or mechanical, including photocopying, recording or by info retrieval system, without prior written permission from the author.

Prospero's Books and Spartan Press would like to thank Jeanette Powers, j.d.tulloch, Jason Preu, M. Scott Douglass, Shawn Pavey, Shaun Savings, Jesse Kates, Jim Holroyd, Steven H.Bridgens, Thomas Mason, Beth Dille, Mason Wolf, The West Plaza Tomato Co., Mark Mclane, the Osage Arts Community and The Robert J. Deuser Foundation For Libertarian Studies.

The author would like to thank the following publications where some of these poems have previously appeared:

"After Hours" *Rockhurst Review,*
"Alone" *The Colour of Saying,* Cross-Cultural Communications, New York, US, *The Seventh Quarry Press*, Swansea, Wales, UK
"Barriers" *The Keep; Radioactive Musings,* UD Press, MO
"Contour Drawings" *Coal City Review*
"Coruscating Cubism" *The Sixth Surface: Steven Holl Lights the Nelson-Atkins Museum,* topo/graphics/press, Kansas City, MO
"Cry Wolf", "Desperation Radio" *The Same*
"Dangling" *The Book of Hopes and Dreams,* Bluechrome Press, UK, and *The Same,* Kansas City, MO
"The Red Sofa," "Dreams of Helgoland" *The Whirlybird Anthology of Kansas City Writers,* Shawnee, KS; *Radioactive Musings,* UD Press, MO
"Guarded Against Visitors" *Runaway Pony: An Anthology of Verse,* Mammoth Press Publications, Lawrence, KS
"Kansas City Renga" Part of *Ghosts Over Water,* Renga Project for *America Now and Here.*

"Media Stake" *Potpourri, Radioactive Musings,* UD Press, MO
"Morning Funeral, Lunch, and Two Weddings" *The Flint Hills Review*, Emporia, KS
"Owl Sounds" *Birds a flight of poems,* The Feral Press, Oyster Bay, New York
"Purple Passion," "Virtual Fame" *Bridging the Waters, An International Bilingual Poetry Anthology,* Co-published by Korean Expatriate Literature & Cross-Cultural Communications, New York, US.
"Radio Renga" *I-70 Review,* Lawrence, KS
"She Sees Elvis Climb the Eiffel Tower," "The Red Sofa," "Roman Dreams" *The Kansas City Star* and John Mark Eberhart's Blog

CONTENTS

Carne Valentine / 1

Media Stake / 2

Connotations / 3

World Capsule / 4

Labyrinths / 5

Cry Wolf / 6

Morning Funeral, Lunch, and Two Weddings / 8

Catching Flies / 11

City Scholar / 12

Batteries (or Special of the Day) / 13

Virtual Fame / 14

Purple Passion / 15

The Red Sofa / 16

Straw Hat Dreams / 17

Dreams of Helgoland / 18

Memphis / 20

She Sees Elvis Climb The Eiffel Tower / 22

Roman Dreams / 24

Graz City Gate / 25

Alone / 26

Wily Birds / 27

Nursing the House / 28

Wrenches / 30

The Ladder Acrobat / 31

The Performer / 32

Doodles / 33

Green Monkeys / 34

Dangling / 35

Give It Up / 36

The Joys of Flight / 37

Owl Sounds / 38

Original Deposit / 39

Lances and Other Sports Heroes / 40

Desperation Radio / 41

Coruscating Cubism / 42

Radio Renga / 43

Kansas City Renga / 44

Junk Mail World / 45

Hidden Castles / 46

Do Today / 47

Barriers / 48

Guarded Against Visitors / 50

Contour Drawings / 51

Replicas / 52

Masonry / 53

Open Mike at the Westsider / 54

Weekend Hells Angels / 56

After Hours / 57

For Dave Paarmann
and all my supportive friends

Carne Valentine

Fat Tuesday
or the end of carnival,
Mardi Gras and national primaries
share the season
of costumed circus participants.
Some sport blue suits and ties,
others don jester costumes
more fitting for the
political spectacle
of ruffled feathers and
stale repertoire.

The drama unfolds
on media screens
where some actors forget to
invent new lines and
repeat their lines in an
endless loop, like
most individuals sans fresh ideas.
Still others with scant support for
pathological ideas
amp up the volume,
repeat lines to silence others,
or
point and shoot to
make their point.

Media Stake

We used to watch witches go up
in flames
to quickly
burn down the fear of darkness
in us

Now
we turn on the TV
open the paper
listen to the radio

Terre Haute
misnomer
for low grounds
slowly
numbing fear
within us
with
sodium pentothal
pancuronium bromide
and
potassium chloride.

Connotations

Some words carry heavy
burdens like
the German word for leader,
Führer.
Consequently, I choose
Leiter for leader in my translation
from English into German.
Just like the English version for
mein Vaterland,
my homeland,
makes me bristle from past connotations
as homeland security
echoes historical commands
of history's despots.

Unfortunate word choices
conjure connotations of conquests
of native lands.

World Capsule

Bee bomb sniffers for home-
land securities
wouldn't be practical for police, but
could work in airports.

The last space shuttle lifts off
for outer space
approaching an outer-worldly structure
built by taught inter-
rational co-
operation.

First we warn teachers to quit teaching,
then we give them a beating,
then we kill them,
because they spread insurgency against
the belief,
the tali-
ban.

No building ban in Shanghai
it adds a city the size of Atlanta
every few years
and
builds the tallest sky-
scrapers.

Watch out for
swarms of killer bees!

Labyrinths

--Inspired by Labyrinth by Robert Morris
at The Nelson Atkins Museum of Art

The crowded glass labyrinth reminds me
of transparent zigzag line partitions
at airport terminals
created to move hapless travellers
toward body-scanners,
or pat-downs, without choice
but to follow a single path,
trudging along a singular path.

Labyrinths are not mazes
labyrinths draw us into a dead-end center
force us to re-trace our steps
repeat our moves.

Mazes confuse with complex choices
fewer are willing to enter
opaque mazes.

Cry Wolf

--Inspired by sculpture Howl by Luis Jiménez 1986

Lavender and slate
plastic fiber
re-enforced
shimmering wolf
bares his teeth
arches his neck
as if howling to a moonworld —

his undulating tail
rippling waves
naked scream
spouting from
his protruding ribs —
hungry
like the *Howl*
of a poet
starving hysterical naked
looking for impossible
fiber in a plastic moonworld
screaming
about
minds
exposed
lost
in the wail
of
the sirens

of Los Alamos
gobbled up
by Madison avenue

the wolf
crying in the
zoo of reality.

Morning Funeral, Lunch, and Two Weddings

I.
In the morning, with a wind-chill factor of minus ten
the seat warmers in the car keep us toasty,
but the mummified figures in the convertible
ahead of the limo are frozen statues
hunched behind the windshield.

At the top of its license plate
the black limo's LCD screen
flashes red letters in a continuous loop:
Congratulations! Just Married!
Esther Marie and John
Let the Party Begin!
The driver's oversight
makes me smile while
you push the channel changer and find
some good Rock-N-Roll
as we inch along toward the highway
for this somber occasion.

The Sheriff's car leading the procession stops
before turning onto the highway,
and the pack of dogs chasing the procession stops.
A large brown mutt with burrs stuck around its snout
lifts its leg and pisses on the rear right tire
of the Sheriff's car.

We turn onto the highway and
soon arrive at the cemetery.
My stomach growls.
We are told that we would not shoot
any more outdoor scenes,
even though the cold
could easily make us cry.

II.
We drive to the Vici Cafe for lunch
where we study the menu,
even though we have seen it before,
the special items list brings hope in this
chicken-fried chicken or
chicken-fried steak restaurant.
I order an other grilled chicken sandwich
and dream of stir-fry.

III.
Crew members smile as we arrive at the church
to film two weddings and a church service.
One of the bride actors has to leave early,
so we film the second wedding first.
We learn about this shooting change
the last minute and scramble to change
into the right costumes.

IV.
In the evening, we return to the
Vici Cafe where
the wedding reception is held and filmed.
It is our dinner and we get two choices,
chicken-fried chicken or
chicken-fried steak.

As the plates arrive one of the crew members remarks:
Look, corn and white gravy and mashed potatoes,
a plate with no color.

Catching Flies

During summer's mosquito season we
avoid the backyard at dusk
and swing on the front porch,
marginally removed from
nuisances of nature.
We watch for passing cars,
the occasional pedestrian,
chat about the day's events and
enjoy our after dinner glass of wine.

As I pick up my glass a fly floats to the surface,
I take a paper towel and fish out the
nuisance — I have no intention not to finish the wine —
and put the paper towel on the railing
next to the swing.

After a few moments the fly
begins to move:
It's missing a wing, you remark.
No, it's just drunk, look closely.
We watch the fly stagger on the crumbled surface
of the paper towel and are
disappointed after it flies away.

Summer's insects serve a purpose after all.

City Scholar

At the Kansas City Literary Festival,
encircled by white folding chairs,
he stands with one hand braced on the podium
and Erasmus springs to life
with humorous passion.

She sits on one side of the open tent
faces the scholar's side view
and the Swarovski storefront behind him
with its *Sex and the City* display.

Erasmus chuckles
as he contemplates the
crystal powers of life.

Batteries
(or Special of the Day)

Would you like some batteries with that?
asks the clerk at the drugstore
as you put various toiletries onto the counter.
With a puzzled expression on your face
that makes me chuckle you reply:
No thank you, this will be all.

She catches me off guard when she asks
if I'd like some batteries with my Swiss cheese.
She cannot possible think
that they are needed for the cheese.

After all of us travelers pile back into
the Jeep I mention the batteries
and Doug explains that clerks
at this drugstore are
required to mention the special of the day
each time they ring up a customer,
or the customer can have the batteries
free of charge.

Marketing at its finest.

Virtual Fame

In the future everyone will be world famous for 15 minutes.

--Andy Warhol

Reality television
gives us famous chefs
touting nutritious
satisfying meals in a jiffy.
Famous, or want to be famous designers
create fashion plates
with flattering garments
chosen for the dowdy
yearning for style.
Experts promise
team effort solutions
for any imaginable ailment
or shortcoming.
Team-effort-weight-loss,
wrinkle loss
anxiety loss,
social ineptitude loss.

Un-famous people eager
to star for free in virtual reality
in cost-effective reality shows,
text details of un-famous facts to producers,
friends and strangers.

Reality television and texting
the opium for the famous
21st century masses.

Purple Passion

Passiflora incarnata of the Passifloraceae family
–This plant may become invasive in some regions or habitats.

USDA

In the Middle Ages
only royals were allowed,
or probably could afford
to don robes of purple:
Tyrian purple
from mollusks of the genus *Murex,*
a pricey dye.

As a teen I shrank from the
regal hue rarely seen in nature.
As a young adult I still avoided the
mixture of red and blue,
preferring attention getting red,
or unobtrusive shades of blue.
Red passion thoughts became
more alluring than purple thoughts
of life's bruises.

Full grown, purple passion's
ripe sophistication invades,
as I wear the purple sweater,
drink the purple passion cocktail.

The Red Sofa

Tired of the hotel's restaurant fare
we slip through its revolving door
and lollygag around the French Quarter
in search of culinary promise.

We linger in front of
a furnishings storefront
admire the sleek design of a curvy red sofa:
After a couple of weeks of looking at that
in your living room
you'll want to take it outside and shoot it!
blurts the bag lady
pushing her cart past us.
Startled, we laugh and stroll off.

Today, leaning back on my red sofa
the middle-aged bag lady plops down
next to me and
warns about summer's curvy
French Quarter
al fresco feasts …

Straw Hat Dreams

At the Writers Place library
a straw hat sits on the shelf above
the open door.
It floats like
a rubber raft on the surface of
a large pool at
a Caribbean resort.

Across the street
snowflakes twirl in
the February wind.

Dreams of Helgoland

In the play
Copenhagen
actors playing
Heisenberg and Bohr
discuss excursions to
Helgoland

and I wander toward
my childhood
and my father's stories of his youth
as a *Matrose* — a sailor.

After the start of the
second World War
there was no civilian German
fleet left. Merchant ships became rescue and
spy ships
under the command of the German Navy.
However, my father insisted that
he was always a civilian sailor on a trade ship,
an Austrian whose rescue ship —
ein Lazarettschiff — sank
during the Allied bombing of Hamburg.

He told stories about travels to places like
Trondheim and Helgoland where
Heisenberg conceived his
quantum mechanics breakthrough in 1925.

Heisenberg and Bohr discuss
nuclear fission in 1941's Copenhagen,
and a *Lazarettschiff* cruises the harbor.

Memphis

We pose in front of the fake gate mural —
the snapshot is free with admission to Graceland —
a welcome distraction while
queuing among a medley of languages
chattering tourists.
After the snapshot
we are jostled on,
guides ask *what language*
while they program
headsets for the tour.
I ask for German for
papa's headset.

After being driven across the street —
it isn't recommended to cross on foot —
and through the actual gate,
I ponder ancient Memphis
on the Nile;
it means a great city.
Memphis on the Mississippi
sports an *Ersatz* pyramid
but boasts a legend.

I cringed as we picked up the 5 by 7 inch snap-
shot — ready in a clear plastic baggy
with a couple of key chain versions tossed in —
but the snapped impression lingers
after papa's visit from Graz
on the Mur river.

Not everything is *Ersatz*
at Graceland.

She Sees Elvis Climb The Eiffel Tower

The metal steps echo
beneath her anxious feet
as she climbs
to view the city from its pinnacle.
Years melt into wrought-iron rafters
as her thoughts shake the hands of those
who lingered here — Hemingway, Stein —
and those she'd known during her interval
in the bright city.

Here
she embraced the man from America,
followed to his land.
Red faded into gray,
she forsook him.
But
not the land:
Drawn by the neon lights of Las Vegas
Drawn by the glamour of Hollywood movies
Drawn by *Viva Las Vegas* — in which
Elvis shakes his hips
surrounded by tall dancers
in fluffy feather and sequin costumes.

Now
she looks down from the pinnacle
at people the height of Leprechauns

waiting at the pylons supporting the tall iron rafters —
doesn't dare linger long,
briskly descends the steps where she sees Elvis climb,
reach the top,
slip and fall —
blinded by the neon lights.

Roman Dreams

The Colosseum beckons my thoughts
with *Roman Fever* where
la dolce vita seems a possibility
(at least for a few days).
I dream of Michelanglo
and want to see
the Sistine Chapel fresco
where Michelangelo labored
for years to earn his keep.
Longing to carve the sculptures of his passion
he painted his fame.

The keyboard of my passion
echoes the satire of being
strolling along the Piazza Navona
while downloading the image of
Bernini's *Fontana Dei Quattro Fiumi.*

The fountain of the four rivers —
Danube, Ganges, Rio della Plata, Nile —
mirrors my image
reflected against   my computer's screen.

Graz City Gate
Das Paulustor

Unchanged it looms,
a guardian of the old
city center.
Medieval sentinel next to
the ugly
electric steel and glass
parking gate.

Often,
I'd passed through this
weighted gate.
Supposedly,
it locked out the Turks
but unlocks the lock
to childhood
images who
snake themselves past my
resistance.

Alone

Inspired by The Hunchback in the Park by Dylan Thomas

Barely noticed, except by children
who ridicule the hunched stature
for his odd demeanor
of imaginative fancies

the poet roams the park
his home and companion
in lonely endeavors.

He struggles against
life's constant din
to contemplate his purpose
in the puzzle of life.

Only unruly children dare to
follow him into the dark
confines of the world's brambles.

Wily Birds

Some are like birds
with clipped wings
who never learned to fly
of their own volition.
Others are like birds of prey
consuming the blood
and energy of others
to serve their own
will and purpose.

Guard against these birds
to soar in your fragile garden of life.

Nursing the Home

*Let's use wood flooring for
the ceiling,
it'll look sharp.*

*Yes, that's a good solution for
the dining room ceiling.
It'll be easy to remove boards if we
have an other plumbing leak.*
Rusty water seeping
blood from old pipes.

We push and cajole wooden planks into place,
fit tongues into grooves and groan as we
stand on ladders to install our new ceiling.
We disagree about methods
but keep on fitting and straining our necks.

Admiring our stately new ceiling we smile,
drive to the hardware store to find new fittings
for the chandelier to attach
to our gleaming
new floor ceiling.

We need a longer metal
rod to hang the light fixture from
and rummage through numerous
little drawers

stuffed with screws, washers,
and nuts,
discover the right section,
the drawers labeled
Lamp Nipples.

The chandelier's dangling glow
is nourishment for tired muscles.

Wrenches

Car wrenches and
gut wrenches
are common.
I glance at the garden
gate. It is closed.
It's the way it can
be
when least ex-
pected.

The next door neighbor's
gate is open and I
stroll right through
because
wrenches quickly
become tools
to adjust the next
open gate.

The Ladder Acrobat
for Diether

First comes the selection:
aluminum or wooden ladder,
and then the needed size.
The wooden ladder is heavier,
the aluminum ladder lighter
with a higher point of gravity …

Lighter is better
and who ever reads the instruction manual.

The plaster cast needs to
be worn for three more weeks.

The Performer

He enters the room
walks along the *edge*
of the world
to the stage
of his world
and
plays to the strings of his guitar.

Doodles

The puffy fellow
runs along the sidewalk
and smiles at us
from the cosmos comic page.

We select the doodles
of life's given choices:
Puffy jolly guy
strolling with friends,
nervous gal
teetering along the
sidewalk on six inch heels
on a lonely sidewalk,
hampered
never running along the
free space
of a self-created path.

Green Monkeys

After Green Monkeys by Dave Paarmann

Green monkeys
jump in caged squares
of dark matter
of a space wave
universe
of signals lost in
curves and crannies
of white space
dotted with red splatters
of golden globe
where shadowy humans
are scattered in a
chaotic mosaic
inhabited by solitary age defying
shorts clad jogger

sprinting toward
the inevitable sunless curves
of gravity.

Dangling

Die Seele baumeln lassen
To let the soul dangle
father would say
as he sat
watching the fountain spurt
water onto
the beach pebbles.

She sits next to the fountain,
eyes glued onto
gray pages of a textbook
she scribbles lists with her fountain-
pen
for tomorrow.

Tomorrow,
she will
dive into
the mist of a gurgling brook

tomorrow
she may
dangle.

Give It Up
after Gibs auf! by Kafka

The morning streets are
empty like the aimless
travel of *Menschen*
who chase after lost minutes.
She notices that her watch
must have stopped during
the night because
the tower clock
indicates it is later than expected.
She starts running
towards the pealing clock
and tries to reach the manor behind
the clock tower that keeps most at bay.

Stop running after
the train that already left the station.

The Joys of Flight

Arrive early for check-in
for a briefer line
during peak travel hours.
Check baggage.
It's worth the extra fee
not to lug anything more than a
little shoulder-bag
through security,
and to avoid squeezing bags
into fought over
overhead compartments.

Bring an actual book that requires
no charging while en route,
because the charging stations
are crowded with travelers
lost without electronic
umbilical cords.

Be happy you arrive at your destination
reasonably on schedule,
even when your luggage doesn't.
After all, as one highly professional
burly male flight attendant
once told his weary travelers:
*Well, at least we got you here
in one piece!*

Be thankful for it.

Owl Sounds

Forced to listen to the radio ads
while he lifts weights at the gym
the sales pitches amuse him:

— *Come to Hooters because*
we have the prettiest girls ....
— *Cosentino's Market has the best*
meats in town.
— *If you have trouble with*
your car's transmission
come to Frank's repair shop ....
— *If you have trouble keeping an erection*
try Viagra and let the dance begin.

After the workout,
starving ...
he rushes to the pharmacy
to hoot like the owls
after dark.

Original Deposit

She asserts that when plaintiff delivered his sperm, it was a gift ....
There was no agreement that the original deposit would be
returned upon request.

—The Associated Press, February 25, 2005

She strolls into his office
smiles at him and
easily becomes his special aide
like Monica — the political aide.

She ponders his deposit,
and uses it for her
special vaginal deposit,
to earn her
baby interest.

He never imagined the
high percent
child interest rate
she would demand
for his professional deposit.

After all,
he never vested
himself at all.

Lances and Other Sports Heroes

I saw Armstrong's face looming large
on the American Century tower
across from the Plaza library
where I listened to *Death of a Salesman*.

I saw his yellow tricot
zip by on the *Champs d'Élysées*.

I saw his bike up close after
he flew into Graz for a mere afternoon
to participate in its old town race
along narrow cobblestone streets
where I ran to grade school.

Former teammate George Hincapie
races and wins
the inaugural Tour of Missouri
lancing inflated tires
of an other strong arm pharmaceutical hero of the defunct
discovery channel team.

Desperation Radio

Desperation Radio,
the letters on the CD
at the shoulder of the road
catch my attention
as we stroll past.
Who tossed it out of a car window?
Who lost it strolling past?

Desperation,
radio the end,
or just a lost CD.
Years ago
the poor citizens
were pushed to
the shoulders of
New Orleans' roadways,
only to bob to the surface on
Katrina's watery swirls.

Coruscating Cubism

Defused
 perspective-defying
  edges
   cascade
    along the
austere symmetry of the neoclassical
facade of the *Met of the Midwest*—
the LINIT channel-glass-edged cubes
are the uncurled forms of its ionic
columns.

Meandering
        along the path that
skirts the iceberg fragments
of the Bloch building

I stop at
Cragg's Turbo swirl
nestled among the perspective-defying
tossed skyscraper
and sense its irregular energy

as I glance at Di Suvero's
Rumi
pointing its orange
steel beam at the future
reassembling vibrations of light.

Radio Renga

Late summer morning tunes
daybreak snoozers' heads
rouse fertile dream pillows.

Radio fusion wave-casts
swinging porch-chairs in the sun.

Remiss tornado funnels
behind brick walls
conceal swinging forecasts.

Blue note news hum local blues
stir buzzing hornet nests.

Kansas City Renga

Magnolia tree blooms
sigh beneath spring snow blanket.
Kansas City April

foolishness snickers at city
squirrels digging bulbs, urban

garden booty. Satur-
day evening's Westport pub
patrons mingle at

windblown restaurant patios
listen to local music.

Junk Mail World

Every day, I am looking for a message
from you in my inbox
or a card in my mailbox,
but find only
spam and envelopes begging for cash,
or bills I hate to pay.

It's a junk mail world we live in,
it's a junk mail world.

Why are you ghosting me,
we had a good time not so long ago.
It's a junk mail
instant message world
where you can hit delete
and never find a note.

It's a junk mail world we live in,
it's a junk mail world.

We un-friend people
like instant messages on our cells
and wonder why we fail
to keep the friends we need.

It's a junk mail world we live in,
it's a junk mail world.

Hidden Castles

Raindrops on turret
dark clouds loom in a brain
attack dark castles

clouds emit rain
in a brain full of armor
to feed the anger

armor clad knights
prevent hordes of peasants
breaching murky moat.

Do Today

Write a new
poem

One that
provides
deep insight

One that
probably
is in first person
recounting
personal flaws

One that
invokes
other's sympathy

One that
does not
offend
anyone's beliefs.

In other words,
write one like most
published
in most glossy magazines.

Barriers

> *Something there is that doesn't love a wall,*
> *That sends the frozen-ground-swell under it,*
> *And spills the upper boulders in the sun,*
> *And makes gaps even two can pass abreast.*
>
> —Robert Frost

Romans built Hadrian's Wall to keep out
the barbarians of northern Britain
but eventually the barbarians —
Picts and Scots —
breached the wall,
adding Great to Britain.
Nevertheless Scots ponder separation
and built their separate
assembly-policy-wall.

Legislators propose to build
an invisible electronic fence
along our border with Mexico,
capture illegals with electronic eyes
across the pared *casa* of America.

The Great Wall of China seen
from outer space
is small,
electronic messages
float past firewalls invisibly
through space.

What is that makes us want a wall?
Building one around Gaza
to keep peoples apart   hide
behind an attempt for peace
because fences make for fenced out neighbors.

I pet my piece of the Berlin Wall.

Guarded Against Visitors
After Looking South by Thomas Weso

Serrated rocks of
fiery tongues
reach like an open multi-thumped
hand into a purple
bruised sky.

Fiery formations merge
to create shadow canyons
that entice
with north of the border
welcoming decks.

Split-rail white image fences
guardrail against shadowy
southern border lurkers
fueled by immigration
media hype.

Contour Drawings
In Memory of Julia Nichols — Daughter of Elizabeth Layton

From the beginning the lines
of your face were drawn
in dark pencil
on thin paper.

Lines, etched deep
by a mother's
struggle to keep from sinking.
You forced yourself
to smile,
wrinkles framing your eyes.

Gazing at your drawings
you unearthed too many lines,
chose to erase your furrows
with carbon monoxide.

Your contours
couldn't save you,
the lines cut too deep.

Replicas

Las Vegas is a city
built of oversized replicas,
a *Maximundus* of the world's trophies
like many of its visitors,
lured by supersize me ads
of an insatiable world.

Minimundus
in Klagenfurt, Austria
has miniature versions
of the Eiffel Tower,
the Taj Mahal
and the leaning tower of Pisa.

The world's wonders
scaled to its visitors.

Masonry

Slowly you cut slabs
while I move jagged chunks
cluster granite and slate for
our front porch puzzle.
You trim some corners for a perfect fit
while I position the pieces
to complete the picture
as we strive for
the right mix of mortar
to cement our patchwork.

Open Mike at the Westsider

We listen to Eddie Delahunt's
Irish tunes nibbling on dinner,
an advantage of
early evening performances.

During Eddie's scheduled set
we watch a number of
musicians stream in through the backdoor.
After a pause we notice a sign-up sheet
and an announcer. A man seated next to us
records musicians with a large video camera.

The hillbilly — at least he dresses the part —
sings with a twang,
but I am not sure that he isn't
a suburb dropout.

The dandy sporting a tux
and his date in a short black dress and stilettos.
His tunes are quite catchy
and he knows how to perform
the part of a big band leader.

The aging hippie with his headband look
and acoustic guitar wants to be Dylan;
and I notice the guy in a plaid shirt
who could be Frank O'Hara's brother.

Frank O'Hara the New York School poet and art lover
who came to his demise on Fire Island,
frolicking on a dune buggy.

This medley of musicians
frolics to its own tunes
for our evening's entertainment.

Weekend Hells Angels

Bike enthusiasts gather at the upscale
local coffee shop patio
at the Country Club Plaza —
Kansas City Missouri's
pedestrian-friendly retail and dining district.
Only sunny days lure riders
who wear Italian leather, sip lattes
and discuss the *raison d'être*
of their middle-aged suburban existence.
Most of the gleaming machines
lined up neatly against the sidewalk's curb
sport Johnson County Kansas plates.

After Hours

I imagine facing Mona Lisa
Da Vinci's masterpiece sans sweaty bodies
like a poem without stanzas:
uninterrupted, smiling only for me.

Silvia Kofler is a widely published poet, translator, educator, and occasional actor who likes to read her work and translations in many places. She has read at New York's Poet's House, the Sacramento Poetry Center, and at Schokoladen in Berlin, Germany. Some of her recent publications include poetry and translations published in *The Colour of Saying, an anthology in celebration of Dylan Thomas by Cross-Cultural Communications, USA, and The Seventh Quarry Press, Wales*. German translations of 10 Hafez ghazals in collaboration with Bill Wolak and Mahmood Karimi-Hakak appeared in *THOSE WHO STOOD UP FOR TOLERANCE DIEJENIGEN DIE FÜR TOLERANZ STANDEN*, published by The Feral Press, NY. She is the editor and publisher of Thorny Locust.

This project was made possible, in part, by generous support from the Osage Arts Community.

Osage Arts Community provides temporary time, space and support for the creation of new artistic works in a retreat format, serving creative people of all kinds — visual artists, composers, poets, fiction and nonfiction writers. Located on a 152-acre farm in an isolated rural mountainside setting in Central Missouri and bordered by ¾ of a mile of the Gasconade River, OAC provides residencies to those working alone, as well as welcoming collaborative teams, offering living space and workspace in a country environment to emerging and mid-career artists. For more information, visit them at osageac.org

www.ingramcontent.com/pod-product-compliance
Lightning Source LLC
Chambersburg PA
CBHW021451080526
44588CB00009B/793